CONTEMPORARY AMERICAN
SUCCESS STORIES

Famous People of
Hispanic Heritage

Volume I

Barbara J. Marvis

A Mitchell Lane
Multicultural Biography Series
• Celebrating Diversity •

CONTEMPORARY AMERICAN SUCCESS STORIES
Famous People of Hispanic Heritage

VOLUME I

Geraldo Rivera
Melissa Gonzalez
Federico Peña
Ellen Ochoa

VOLUME II

Tommy Nuñez
Margarita Esquiroz
Cesar Chavez
Antonia Novello

VOLUME III

Giselle Fernandez
Jon Secada
Desi Arnaz
Joan Baez

VOLUME IV

Nancy Lopez
Joseph Unanue
Pedro José Greer
Hilda Perera

VOLUME V

Tomas Rivera
Selena Quintanilla Perez
Sandra Cisneros
Julio Cesar Chavez

VOLUME VI

John Leguizamo
Vikki Carr
Ricardo Montalbán
Raquel Welch

VOLUME VII

Tony Perez
Rosie Perez
Lourdes G. Baird
Jaime Escalante

VOLUME VIII

Gloria Estefan
José Serrano
Lynda Carter
Jesse Treviño

Illustrated by Barbara Tidman
Cover illustration by Barbara Tidman
Project Editor: Susan R. Scarfe
Library of Congress Catalog Card Number: 95-75963

Mitchell Lane
PUBLISHERS
Your Path To Quality Educational Material

ISBN 1-883845-21-1 hardcover
ISBN 1-883845-20-3 softcover

TABLE OF CONTENTS

Acknowledgments

Every reasonable effort has been made to seek copyright permission, where such permission has been deemed necessary. Any oversight brought to the publisher's attention will be corrected in future printings.

Most of the stories in this series were written through personal interviews and/or with the complete permission of the person, representative of, or family of the person being profiled and are authorized biographies.

We wish to acknowledge with gratitude the generous cooperation of Geraldo Rivera (telephone interview March 20, 1995), Jo-Ann Torres Conte, and Erica Pressman in the compilation of the story about and photographs of Geraldo Rivera; Melissa Gonzalez (telephone interview March 9, 1995), Everlidis Rojas, Mickey Grossman, Gigi Harris Faraci, Carolyn Miller, and Caroline Mendoza for their help with our story and photographs of Melissa Gonzalez; Federico Peña (telephone interview April 27, 1995), Lenny Glynn, Ronda Jackson, Alexander Elles-Boyle, and Barbara Baldwin for supplying information and photographs about Federico Peña; and Ellen Ochoa (telephone interview April 6, 1995), Kyle Herring, and Lucy Lytwinsky for their help with our story about Ellen Ochoa. We also wish to express our sincere thanks to Elaine DagenBela of the Hispanic Heritage Awards for her help with recommendations for those to be included in this series.

Photograph Credits

The quality of the photographs in this book may vary; many of them are personal snapshots supplied to us courtesy of the person being profiled. Many are very old, one-of-a-kind photos. Most are not professional photographs, nor were they intended to be. The publisher felt that the personal nature of the stories in this book would only be enhanced by real-life, family-album-type photos, and chose to include many interesting snapshots, even if they were not quite the best quality.

p.11 courtesy Jo-Ann Torres Conte; p.13, p.15, p.16, p.17, p.30, p.39 courtesy Geraldo Rivera Collection; p.40, p.41 courtesy Tribune Entertainment; p.42, p.44 Geraldo Rivera Collection; p.45 courtesy Tribune Entertainment; p.49, p.50, p.51, p.52, p.54 top and bottom, p.55 courtesy Everlidis Rojas; p.56 top and bottom, p.57 courtesy Children's Television Workshop; p.58 courtesy Everlidas Rojas; p.59 courtesy Children's Television Workshop; p.71 UPI/Bettmann; p73, p.75, p.77 Department of Transportation; p.83 NASA; p.84, p.86 courtesy Rosanne Ochoa; p.88, p.90, p.91, p.92, p.93 NASA.

INTRODUCTION

Kathy Escamilla

One of the fastest growing ethno-linguistic groups in the United States is a group of people who are collectively called Hispanic. The term *Hispanic* is an umbrella term that encompasses people from many nationalities, from all races, and from many social and cultural groups. The label *Hispanic* sometimes obscures the diversity of people who come from different countries and speak different varieties of Spanish. Therefore, it is crucial to know that the term *Hispanic* encompasses persons whose origins are from Spanish-speaking countries, including Spain, Mexico, Central and South America, Cuba, Puerto Rico, the Dominican Republic, and the United States. It is important also to note that Spanish is the heritage language of most Hispanics. However, Hispanics living in the United States are also linguistically diverse. Some speak mostly Spanish and little English, others are bilingual, and some speak only English.

Hispanics are often also collectively called Latinos. In addition to calling themselves Hispanics or Latinos, many people in this group also identify themselves in more specific terms according to their country of origin or their ethnic group (e.g. Cuban-American, Chicano, Puerto Rican-American, etc.) The population of Hispanics in the United States is expected to triple in the next twenty-five years, making it imperative that students in schools understand and appreciate the enormous contributions that persons of Hispanic heritage have made in the Western Hemisphere in general and in the United States in particular.

There are many who believe that in order to be successful in the United States now and in the twenty-first century, all persons from diverse cultural backgrounds, such as Hispanics, should be assimilated. To be assimilated means losing one's distinct cultural and linguistic heritage and changing to or adopting the cultural attributes of the dominant culture.

Others disagree with the assimilationist viewpoint and believe that it is both possible and desirable for persons from diverse cultural backgrounds to maintain their cultural heritage and also to contribute positively and successfully to the dominant culture. This viewpoint is called cultural pluralism, and it is from the perspective of cultural pluralism that these biographies are written. They represent persons who identify strongly with their Hispanic heritage and at the same time who are proud of being citizens of the United States and successful contributors to U.S. society.

The biographies in these books represent the diversity of Hispanic heritage in the United States. Persons featured are contemporary figures whose national origins range from Argentina to Arizona and whose careers and contributions cover many aspects of contemporary life in the United States. These biographies include writers, musicians, actors, journalists, astronauts, businesspeople, judges, political activists, and politicians. Further, they include Hispanic women and men, and thus characterize the changing role of all women in the United States. Each person profiled in this book is a positive role model, not only for persons of Hispanic heritage, but for any person.

Collectively, these biographies demonstrate the value of cultural pluralism and a view that the future strength of the United States lies in nurturing the diversity of its human potential, not in its uniformity.

Dr. Kathy Escamilla is currently Vice President of the National Association for Bilingual Education and an Associate Professor of Bilingual Education and Multicultural Education at the University of Colorado, Denver. She previously taught at the University of Arizona, and was the Director of Bilingual Education for the Tucson Unified School District in Tucson, Arizona. Dr. Escamilla earned a B.A. degree in Spanish and Literature from the University of Colorado in 1971. Her master's degree is in bilingual education from the University of Kansas, and she earned her doctorate in bilingual education from UCLA in 1987.

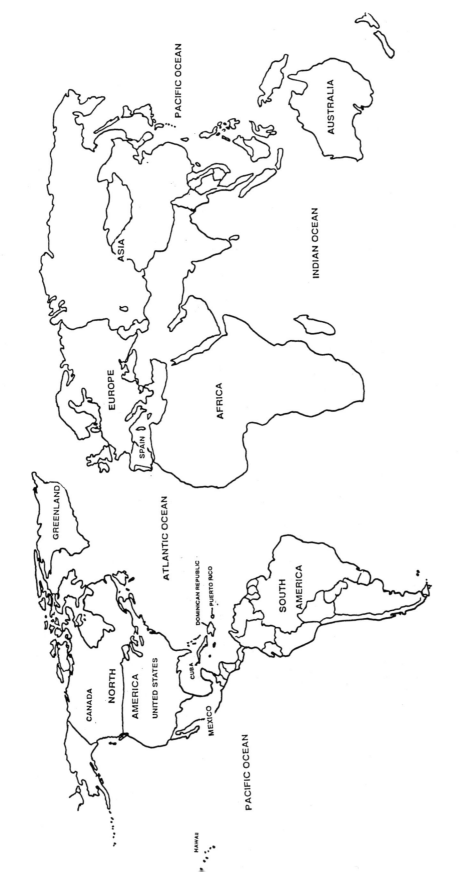

MAP OF THE WORLD

GERALDO RIVERA

Broadcast Journalist, Investigative Reporter, Talk-Show Host
1943-

"**M**y advice to young minorities is just this: 'Yes, the world is unfair; there is racism and discrimination. Just because you are starting out with a strike or two against you, don't let that get you down. Fight against it. Don't feel sorry for yourself. Above all, stay in school. Education is the great equalizer. Even if you never get in the country club, you'll be just as smart, just as educated as anyone else – and that's what gives you options; that's what gives you opportunities. The better you do in school, the better it is for your future . . . Education is your ticket out of wherever you want to leave.' "

Geraldo Rivera, as told to Barbara Marvis, March 1995

BIO HIGHLIGHTS

- Born July 4, 1943; mother: Lilly Friedman; father: Cruz Rivera
- Grew up on Long Island, New York
- Earned law degree from Brooklyn Law School
- Passed New York Bar and went to work for Community Action for Legal Services
- Discovered by local ABC news affiliate in New York in 1970
- Helped launch prime-time news magazine *20/20* in 1978
- Launched talk show *Geraldo* in 1987
- Host of CNBC commentary *Rivera Live* in 1994
- Currently: married to C. C. Dyer; they have two daughters, Isabella and Simone; son Gabriel from a previous marriage

> "So, all at once, I blurted out, 'If you stay in school and graduate, I'll finance your college education.' All of a sudden, I had their attention."

GERALDO RIVERA

In 1989, well-known broadcast journalist Geraldo Rivera spoke to an eighth-grade class from Junior High School 45 in East Harlem in New York City. As part of Mayor Koch's request that he and other role models "adopt" a class in some of the city's most economically disadvantaged areas, Geraldo showed up to give a motivational speech about the rewards of staying in school. "I told them they could be successes, just like me," he says, "and they looked at me like I was speaking a different language. They certainly did not accept the fantasy of the American dream. These were not youngsters who were starting out with just one or two strikes against them. These were not children with the usual teenage problems or a simple lack of interest in school. Some of them had parents with their own agenda and no interest in their children's lives. Some of them had no parents at all. They lived in some of the worst neighborhoods in America. Many of them were part of the welfare system. But here I was trying to convince them they had a reason to stay in school, and I was not getting any reaction. So, all at once, I blurted out, 'If you stay in school and graduate, I'll finance your college education.' All of a sudden, I had their attention . . .

"There were twenty-four students in that eighth-grade class. I visited them several times a year. It was very difficult just getting them to finish high school in a school district where less than half the students graduate and less than ten percent go on to college. In 1990, I set up the Maravilla Foundation for this class, and by June 1993 there were fifteen students still in our program. Eleven of these graduated from high school that June. As of

1995, we have a core group of eleven students in the Foundation in their second year of college. I have funded their education with the proceeds from my autobiography, *Exposing Myself* [published in 1991 by Bantam Books]. It's been a long, hard road, but these young adults have become a part of my family."

Geraldo Rivera, whose genuine desire to "make a difference," and whose big-hearted generosity has received considerably less press than

Pictured with Geraldo and the First Lady of Puerto Rico, Maga Rosello, are eight of the eleven students currently attending college, funded by the Maravilla Foundation.

the topics of most of his talk shows, was not born with a silver spoon in his mouth, either. He had to win his success the hard way: he had to earn it.

Born on the stroke of midnight that hailed in the Fourth of July in 1943, Gerald Riviera was the oldest of four children born to Cruz Rivera and Lilly Friedman. His two sisters, Irene and Sharon, and his younger brother Craig, eleven years his junior, grew up on Long Island. About the time that Craig was born, his parents also adopted Willie, a cousin from Puerto Rico. Their mother, attempting to cover up their ethnic background, spelled their father's surname with an extra *i* on three of her four children's birth certificates. This confused the entire family. When Lilly was asked about the inconsistencies, she would joke that she "forgot" how to spell it. Nevertheless, until he was twenty-four, Geraldo was known as Gerry Riviera.

Geraldo's father, born in Puerto Rico, was one of nineteen children born to Juan and Tomasa Rivera. Geraldo's grandfather was a field supervisor on a huge sugar plantation. His grandmother was a loving disciplinarian, who raised not only nineteen of her own children, but also two adopted ones and countless nieces, nephews, and grandchildren. His grandparents were married for more than six decades, and they both

When Cruz married Lilly, he adopted the name Allen in an attempt to become more American for his Jewish in-laws.

lived to be ninety-five. When Cruz came to the United States as a young man, he was filled with boundless energy and dreams of what wonders were held for him in America. Sadly, he never realized all his dreams: he spent much of his working life washing dishes, driving a cab, or supervising the mostly Hispanic staff in the cafeteria kitchen of Republic, a big defense plant on Long Island. Cruz and Lilly met in a cafeteria where they both worked: he washed dishes and she took care of the counter. When he married Lilly, Cruz adopted the name Allen in an attempt to become more American for his Jewish in-laws. Geraldo tells us that Lilly's parents were so appalled that their daughter had married a Puerto Rican, they literally "died of shame" shortly after the wedding.

Geraldo with his family. From left to right: Geraldo, Irene, Craig, their mother, Lillian, Sharon, and Wilfredo, taken in 1989.

Geraldo says that growing up on Long Island was anything but fun. His mother thought her family should have some religious identity, so the family joined the newly established Temple Beth El, where Gerald was bar mitzvahed. It

When he was sixteen, Geraldo went to Puerto Rico to spend the summer with his paternal grandparents. There, he learned to speak Spanish.

seemed he faced racial prejudice from every end. If he wasn't being put down for his Puerto Rican heritage, then he was faced with anti-Semitism from junior Nazi groups. Geraldo remembers an incident in high school when he was dating a lovely Italian girl whose parents forbade her to see him. They were afraid that if they married, they would produce "black" children. In fact, the confusion surrounding the spelling of his last name and his mixed heritage spurred ridiculous stories about his background. In 1973, a New York disc jockey publicly announced that Geraldo was really a Jew posing as a Puerto Rican to take advantage of affirmative action, and that his real last name was Rivers!

When he was ten, Geraldo got his first taste of journalism as a paperboy. He delivered the *Long Island Press.* According to Geraldo, it was a very hard paper to sell. *Newsday* was the best-selling newspaper at the time, and he was delivering the neighborhood's second choice. He learned that it was hard to be in second place. Geraldo always wanted to be number one.

When he was sixteen, Geraldo went to Puerto Rico to spend the summer with his paternal grandparents. There, he learned to speak Spanish, of necessity, and he learned a great deal about his Puerto Rican ancestors. The trip enabled him to deal more effectively with his mixed heritage.

Geraldo attended West Babylon High. He was never sure quite where he belonged. At one end, he was cocaptain of the football team; at the other, he was a member of a little-known street gang called the Corner Boys, who mostly got into fights with kids from neighboring schools. As a result, he did very poorly in school, even though he was quite bright.

He remembers buying his first car, a 1947 Chevy for twenty-five dollars. When he got his car, he dropped the Corner Boys in favor of a new group called the Valve Grinders. Soon, he found himself stealing hubcaps! "I lived the cliché," Geraldo says. "Even in the suburbs, I was a Puerto Rican stealing hubcaps." The car got him into a lot of trouble.

Geraldo with his father in 1949

Even though Geraldo was not always the perfect student while he was in school, he knew the value of an education. He told his friend Frankie DeCecco that the best way to make it in life was to go on to college and then make a lot of money. Frankie thought a good job was to sell cars for a Chevrolet dealership, like his

Geraldo Rivera

Geraldo's high-school yearbook picture (West Babylon High, 1961)

▼▼▼▼▼▼

At college, he told everyone he was Gerry Riviera, son of a well-to-do Spanish merchant.

stepfather did. Geraldo told him that after he went to college, he could own the whole dealership. The two friends made a bet late in high school. Geraldo bet Frankie that in ten years, he'd be making thirty thousand dollars. They were to meet in exactly ten years at the top of the Empire State Building. If Geraldo were making thirty grand, Frankie would buy him dinner. If he had not yet made the grade, dinner would be on Geraldo. By the time that day came, both Frankie and Geraldo were married. Geraldo was already in the television news business and Frankie was still living on Long Island selling cars. Frankie conceded the bet and bought Geraldo dinner.

After high school, Geraldo decided to become a Merchant Marine officer. He managed to get accepted at Fort Schuyler, New York State Maritime College, but he had to take remedial courses in math and English. There he had the prospect of a thrilling career at sea. It was the greatest adventure he could think of at the time. He could earn his college degree, an ensign's commission in the navy reserve, and get a license as a third mate in the merchant fleet. He worked hard at his studies. He started as a goalie for the varsity soccer and lacrosse teams, and he joined the rowing team. At college, he told everyone he was Gerry Riviera, son of a well-to-do Spanish merchant.

Geraldo finds it ironic that he actually sailed across the Atlantic Ocean before he ever crossed the Hudson River to New Jersey. The summer after his freshman year, he sailed aboard the *John Brown*, a converted World War II troop transport, to the Strait of Gibraltar and on to Spain, Italy, Holland, Germany, and Norway. He was fascinated with the sailor's life and determined to make it his life, too. It was never to be, but

he did develop his love of sailing and of the sea from this experience.

Back in college for his second year, his life became a nightmare. An upperclassman picked on him the whole year until he decided to leave Fort Schuyler. Disappointed at the turn of events, that summer Geraldo set out with his friend Frankie for the West Coast. He decided that the University of Arizona at Tucson was the place for him to finish his educa-

Geraldo, in center of picture, at Fort Schuyler

"Let's both get married," Vic suggested. "You marry your girl, I'll marry mine."

tion. He was quickly accepted, and he and Frankie traveled to California to have some fun for the rest of the summer.

At a campus party during his senior year, Geraldo met Linda Coblentz, who was a transfer student from North Carolina and an artist. Her parents lived in Scottsdale, Arizona. Though marriage was the farthest thing from Geraldo's mind in his senior year, an old high school friend named Vic Furio made him think again. The year was 1965 and the Vietnam War was escalating. When Geraldo left the Maritime College, he also lost all interest in the military. He wanted no part of the war. Draft-dodging at that time was widespread. Both college and marriage were reasons for automatic deferral from the draft. But Geraldo was about to graduate from college and this deferral would be lost. Vic had a wonderful suggestion for avoiding the draft. "Let's both get married," Vic suggested. "You marry your girl, I'll marry mine," he elaborated.

"What'll that do?" Geraldo wondered.

"That will get us an automatic deferral," Vic said. "Then the four of us will travel, or we'll go to Europe to work, or maybe to Africa. By the time they catch up to us, the war will be over."

This strategy made great sense to Geraldo, even though he wasn't sure he wanted to commit himself to one woman. But the thought was exciting. So he asked Linda to marry him. She said yes, and the young couple traveled to Scottsdale to break the good news to Linda's parents. They were somewhat skeptical about this young man who claimed to be the son of a prosperous restaurateur of Spanish descent, bound for glory and adventure abroad. However, Linda's parents gave their blessings and the wedding was set to take place upon graduation. Geraldo never mentioned his ulterior motives to Linda or her parents.

Geraldo then took off for New York to tell his parents of his plans to marry. About a month or two later, Vic called to tell Geraldo that he had changed his mind about getting married and had enlisted in the Marine Corps instead! Geraldo was floored. His wedding was only a week away, and it was too late to back out. This was how Geraldo entered marriage number one, which was doomed to fail even before the marriage certificate was signed.

The wedding took place in Scottsdale, beneath Camelback Mountain. Of his family and close friends, only his sister Sharon could be present on such short notice. Since Vic had backed out of the deal, the couple decided not to travel abroad; instead they headed for sunny California. They bought a 1954 Chevy and

Vic called to tell Geraldo that he had changed his mind about getting married and had enlisted in the Marines Corps instead!

Despite the low rent, the apartment turned out to be expensive for Linda and Geraldo. Their house was robbed several times and they lost everything they owned.

GERALDO RIVERA

headed west, with no long-range plans or visions for their future. Finally, Linda's father suggested that Geraldo might want to do something with his life and said he ought to go to law school. "You have a sharp mind," he told Geraldo. "You're fast on your feet. Why don't you go to law school?"

This seemed like the perfect solution to Geraldo's uncertain future. Geraldo applied and was accepted at Brooklyn Law School. Just after Christmas of 1965, Linda and Geraldo loaded up their old Chevy and left California for New York. The young couple settled in Manhattan on Seventh Street in the East Village. He earned a partial scholarship and did very well in school. But the couple was very poor in those days. They lived in a bad part of town where the rent was cheap. It was all they could afford. Despite the low rent, the apartment turned out to be expensive for Linda and Geraldo. Their house was robbed several times and they lost everything they owned.

Geraldo found part-time work in a department store and Linda waitressed between her classes at the Art Students League. The two never complained about their hardship.

During this time, Geraldo became friends with another law-school student named Danny Goldfarb and with Captain Joseph Allen of the

New York Police Department. Together, the three of them waged their own battle against crime in the city. Geraldo sought and won an internship with the Manhattan District Attorney's office, working underneath Frank Hogan, known as the "mob buster." In the summer of 1967, Geraldo found himself to be a twenty-four-year-old born-again crime-stopper with a vengeance against scumbags. He began the fall semester at Brooklyn Law School near the top of his class.

Nearly two years previous to this, Cruz Rivera had lost his job at Republic, when the food concession was sold to a national restaurant chain. The new management decided that Cruz made too much money and was too old for the job. (He was earning two hundred dollars a week and was fifty years old at the time.) With what savings he had managed to put away over the years, Cruz opened a little coffee shop in a small shopping center near his home. To everyone's surprise, the shop was a success, and Cruz sold it at a profit in 1967. He used the proceeds, plus lots of borrowed money, to purchase a twenty-four-hour restaurant called Midwell Diner. He called the new place Al's Midwell Diner, and worked there eighteen hours a day, seven days a week. It almost killed him. Despite his best efforts, the restaurant never made enough money to pay all the bills and the

▼▼▼▼▼▼
In the summer of 1967, Geraldo found himself to be a twenty-four-year-old born-again crime-stopper.
▲▲▲▲▲▲

Geraldo's marriage to Linda lasted barely two years.

GERALDO RIVERA

loans. Finally, he called his oldest son to ask for his help.

Geraldo, Linda, and their friend Danny were soon helping at the restaurant. Geraldo took over the grill, Linda waitressed, and Danny worked the cash register. Despite their hard work, it was a losing battle. The restaurant finally had to be closed and was sold by bankruptcy court to clear the debts. To add to the misfortunes, Cruz had put up his half of the house as collateral for the loan and the court was about to sell his half interest. Geraldo managed to borrow enough money to save the house.

The only job his father could then find was as a night watchman at a shopping center for very little pay. He was never quite the same after that. Shortly thereafter, Linda and Geraldo broke up, thus ending the first of what would eventually be three failed marriages. This first marriage lasted barely two years. It was also at about this time that Geraldo discovered that his good friend Joey of the NYPD was a rogue cop. He was under investigation for alleged police corruption; he died fifteen years later, a discredit to the field of law enforcement. Geraldo was crushed. At the time, he believed all policemen were good policemen. It was a rude awakening. He always thought that those in law enforcement were the good guys; the scumbags were the evil ones. What he found out about Joey made Geraldo want to be on the good side even more. In his final year at Brooklyn Law, Geraldo became more convinced than ever that he would become a lawyer of and for the people.

Geraldo earned his Juris Doctor in 1969 and graduated fifth in his class of 350 students. Upon graduation, Geraldo was recruited by the University of Pennsylvania, which administered the Reginald Heber Smith Fellowship in Poverty Law. This was a federally funded program designed to train and sponsor poverty lawyers to advocate for the poor. The job paid an annual stipend of ten thousand dollars. Geraldo was assigned to the Community Action for Legal Services (CALS) office in lower Manhattan. For the first time in his life, Geraldo thought he had the perfect job in the perfect setting. He went on to pass the New York State Bar exam, and his life as a professional student finally came to an end.

About this time, Geraldo finally came to terms with his mixed heritage. Although he now readily admits "I am all Puerto Rican and all Jewish," he had decided he was Puerto Rican first and Jewish second. The Jews were a strong people, he reasoned, and they didn't need him. The Puerto Ricans did. He set out to evoke fun-

Upon graduation [from law school], Geraldo was recruited by the University of Pennsylvania, which administered the Reginald Heber Smith Fellowship in Poverty Law.

damental social change. He was out to save the
world. And he actually spent the majority of the
next several decades looking for ways to change
things for the better.

Most of his work for CALS was in housing
court, winning damages for poor tenants against
landlords who violated rent-control laws, in
criminal court defending left-wing radicals accused of harassment or obstruction of justice, and
in civil court representing exploited consumers.
Always quick to fight for the rights of others,
Geraldo enjoyed the adventure and the thrill of
fighting for the oppressed.

In the fall of 1969, Geraldo heard about a Puerto Rican activist group known as the Young
Lords, operating in "El Barrio" in Spanish Harlem. They had been disrupting services at a local church and demanding that the wealthy
members of the church help the poor people in
the nearby neighborhoods. They wanted the
church to be used for daycare, a free-breakfast
program, and an emergency shelter. The church
officials would not agree. Wearing their trade-
mark purple berets, the Young Lords attempted
to take over the church one Sunday. Thirteen
Lords were arrested. Geraldo demanded to represent them. He demanded to be in the middle
of any cause he deemed worthwhile. At the
time, the Young Lords seemed like a worthwhile

cause. Their plight brought sympathetic news coverage, and Geraldo was often interviewed. Wherever people were yelling for their rights, Geraldo was there, yelling the loudest of them all.

When his commitment to CALS was about to expire, Geraldo began to think of another line of work. He felt he could be a very good attorney, but he quickly saw that being a lawyer wasn't about justice at all. "Being an attorney," he now says, "is about winning and losing. I like to win. One of the last clients I defended was accused of rape. Though he never confessed to me that he did it, the evidence indicated that he in fact had. He was ultimately acquitted and went free. I don't think I could have continued to be a lawyer if winning meant I was letting guilty people go free. I feel terrible when justice is not served. I like to champion for the oppressed, for the underdog. But I don't believe that criminals should go unpunished, and I was lucky that my big break in television came along when it did."

In 1970, Gloria Rojas, a local TV reporter, approached Geraldo about a job at WABC-TV, the ABC affiliate in New York City. The news director, Al Primo, was looking to add minorities to his ethnically diverse on-air team. Al convinced Geraldo that he could help his people

"I don't think I could have continued to be a lawyer if winning meant I was letting guilty people go free. I feel terrible when justice is not served."

in bigger and better ways and offered to send him to a crash course in journalism at Columbia University. He also offered a big increase in his salary, and Geraldo couldn't refuse. Those attributes that made Geraldo a good litigator in court would make him a good news reporter as well.

Well-spoken and full of new ideas fueled mostly by his "I don't know any better" demeanor, he changed his name from Gerald to Geraldo and began making news himself. By the time his chapter with ABC News was written some fifteen years later, he had won many awards for his journalism, including two Columbia DuPont journalism awards, two Scripps Howard journalism awards, and the George Foster Peabody Award. He had also become a household name. Filled with what he calls "Puerto Rican compassion mixed with Jewish guilt," Geraldo became the champion of the underdog. But it was not an easy job, especially in the beginning.

During his first day on the job at Channel 7 for *Eyewitness News*, Geraldo was assigned to interview the losing candidate for attorney general in the recent election. Despite his best efforts, none of his interview was aired. Geraldo was crushed. His colleagues at the station assured him that this was not unusual for a new

He changed his name from Gerald to Geraldo.

and inexperienced reporter and it might take some time to actually get his voice or his face on the air. Geraldo was determined that it would not take very long. Within three weeks, he was on the air.

Geraldo was assigned to interview some truant kids, and he got everyone's attention when he sat down on the front stoop to talk with them. Everyone liked his approach, which had never been tried before: talking to the kids on their level. His piece got a lot of attention. Geraldo says he took this approach because he didn't know any better. Overnight, he felt like a star. But this star was knocked out of the sky shortly thereafter when he taped a piece about a condemned tenement in the South Bronx, but went around the corner from the studio to do the lead-in piece. Angry callers resented having their upscale neighborhood implicated in a piece about the South Bronx.

Soon, Geraldo became the man on the streets. He was the ghetto reporter. He did many special reports that won him recognition. "Drug Crisis in East Harlem" won him several awards. Based on his continuing success, he was able to renegotiate his salary several times to reflect his rising stardom. In November 1971, the *New York Times* did a story about him. He wasn't sure just where he was going or where he'd land

▼▼▼▼▼▼
Soon, Geraldo became the man on the streets.
▲▲▲▲▲▲

Geraldo
listened to
what Mike
Wilkins had
to say. He
then
gathered a
camera
crew and,
with
cameras
rolling,
burst into
the facility
unannounced
and
uninvited.

GERALDO RIVERA

when he got there, but the story confirmed he was rising rapidly. Geraldo had it all. He was named Broadcaster of the Year by the New York State Associated Press in 1971, 1972, and again in 1974.

On December 14, 1971, Geraldo married Edie Vonnegut, daughter of famed author Kurt Vonnegut. The wedding took place at the Vonnegut house on Cape Cod, and this time his parents and family were able to attend. Thus began marriage number two. With Edie, he authored several children's books. He wrote, she illustrated. *Miguel Robles – So Far* was published by Harcourt in 1973. *A Special Kind of Courage: Profiles of Young Americans* was published by Simon & Schuster in 1976.

One day in early 1972, Geraldo received a phone call from an acquaintance named Mike Wilkins. Wilkins had just been fired from the Willowbrook State School on Staten Island, the nation's largest facility for the mentally retarded. They operated under the jurisdiction of the New York Department of Mental Hygiene. He was fired, Wilkins told Geraldo, for encouraging parents of the children to unite and lobby for improved living conditions at the facility.

Geraldo listened to what Mike Wilkins had to say. He then gathered a camera crew and, with cameras rolling, burst into the facility unannounced and uninvited. He took footage of many profoundly retarded children living in a ward that looked like an unfinished basement. There were exposed pipes and chunks of fallen plaster. Many of the children were naked; some wore pieces of clothing. Still others were in straitjackets. Most of the children were unattended and many were rolling around on the floor in filth. It smelled of disease and death and Geraldo could not wait to get out of there and expose this atrocity to the public.

This episode followed a long series of specials that Geraldo broadcast in an effort to improve conditions at Willowbrook or to close it down altogether. His special on Willowbrook became the highest rated local news special in the history of TV at that time, and it directly contributed to additional funding for Willowbrook and to its eventual closing fifteen years later. Geraldo also started a special charity called One-to-One, for which he raised money to allow the mentally retarded to live at home or in smaller group homes with some dignity. His Willowbrook special won him his first DuPont Columbia award and brought him much-deserved attention and fame.

Two other documentaries won him critical acclaim. "Migrants – Dirt Cheap" exposed the difficult conditions migrant workers had to face,

He took footage of many profoundly retarded children living in a ward that looked like an unfinished basement.

and "The Littlest Junkie" explored the long road to recovery of babies born to drug-addicted mothers. For "The Littlest Junkie" Geraldo earned his second DuPont Columbia award.

Geraldo began to think he was invincible. In his own words, he says, "I was bigger than the establishment. I was operating on some other,

Geraldo with Bernard Carabello, a former Willowbrook patient; taken in 1993 at the ARC National Convention in Providence, R.I.

higher plane." And so he thought the station rules that forbade the news team from taking part in local politics did not apply to him. In 1972, Geraldo publicly backed George McGovern for

President and agreed to appear at a fund-raising event for him at the Palace Theatre. He was told by his employers not to appear at this public event. But Geraldo did not listen.

"Back then, I was so convinced of my invincibility, and my total independence, and my ability to flout convention and make my own rules, that I made a stand over what should never have been an issue. I didn't belong on the Palace Theatre stage, but I was bullheaded about my right to be there." This was only one of the many run-ins Geraldo would have with network management over the next thirteen years.

The year was only 1972, and already Geraldo was bumping heads with the network brass. By July of 1973, Geraldo had a late-night news magazine that he had invented called *Good Night America*. The show ran with some regularity over the next three years. During these years, Geraldo was integral in instituting the Channel 7 Help Center, the on-air problem-solver for the viewing public. With a small staff of Fordham University law students and some trained volunteers, Geraldo helped fix problems for viewers who wrote or called him. He also did a show for a local radio station during this time.

Geraldo was integral in instituting the Channel 7 Help Center, the on-air problem-solver for the viewing public.

GERALDO RIVERA

By 1974, Edie and Geraldo were divorced. By late 1975, Geraldo was affiliated with the early morning show *Good Morning America*. Channel 7 decided he had too many things going at once and decided to let him go. Geraldo was somewhat taken aback by their decision, though he still had his plate full doing the morning show, the evening show, and the radio programs. But he had lost his connection to the local news, and this was a tough adjustment for him.

Geraldo had formed his own production company, Maravilla Productions, to produce *Good Night America*. By 1975, he was able to help support his parents by giving them jobs there. He joked that his childhood dream was to be mayor of New York City, and for a while there were rumors that he thought of running. But Geraldo says this was not so. It may have been a fleeting thought in his younger days, but he never gave it much thought later on. Besides, he says, at some points in his career, he thought he was more powerful than the mayor.

By New Year's Eve of 1976, Geraldo was married again. This time he married Sheri Braverman, who wanted a divorce after just three weeks! Geraldo tried to work things out, and soon Sheri was managing all of Geraldo's business. She became a great help to Geraldo.

GERALDO RIVERA

Good Night America was taken off the air in June 1977. Geraldo protested very loudly about the demise of the show and was consequently fired from *Good Morning America*, too. But luck was still with Geraldo. Roone Arledge, the new president of ABC News, then hired him for the *Evening News*. Geraldo had finally arrived. He was a network newsman, a position he never thought he could attain. He immediately landed an exclusive interview with Cuban President Fidel Castro.

One short year after *Good Night America* was canceled, Geraldo was in on the launch of a brand-new prime-time news magazine called *20/20*. It premiered on June 6, 1978, and Geraldo was named the chief reporter. Though the initial reviews were not good, the turning point came when Geraldo did a special about the cover-up surrounding Elvis' death. This established the show as a major player. Geraldo eventually would spend seven and a half years on *20/20*, until 1985.

Another big turning point in Geraldo's life came in 1979, when he and Sheri finally had a son, Gabriel. Born on July 2, Gabriel was five weeks early. Gabriel's birth changed Geraldo's outlook on life. At least for a short while, Geraldo just wanted to be close to his wife and son.

Geraldo had finally arrived. He was a network newsman, a position he never thought he could attain.

A big turning point in Geraldo's life came in 1979, when he and Sheri finally had a son, Gabriel.

GERALDO RIVERA

However, Geraldo's family attitudes did not last long, and soon he and Sheri were separated. She took Gabriel to live with her on the West Coast.

The beginning of the end of Geraldo's relationship with ABC News came in 1983 when he did an interview with PLO leader Yasir Arafat. When ABC aired the piece, they cut Geraldo out of all the clips. Geraldo was angry and decided to go on strike. He took C. C. Dyer, his associate producer, with him to Egypt on vacation. He went from being a weekly fixture on *20/20* to being an every-other-month contributor. He had produced thirty-one reports over the preceding ten months, but did only two stories over the next three months. He did all this to make a point and show ABC how much they'd miss him if he were gone. "Unfortunately," Geraldo says, "nobody seemed to care."

His colleague on *20/20*, Barbara Walters, approached him one day about his lengthy absence. She reminded him that his contract had only one year to go until renewal, and unless he wanted to lose his job, he had better think of going back to work. She was right. Even though Geraldo wanted to make a point, he could not afford to lose his job. By this time, he was making a lot of money, over one million dollars a year. And he had spent nearly all of it. Of course he still had to support Sheri, whom he was in the process of divorcing, and Gabriel, and he was supporting his parents, also. Over the years, as his salary grew, he developed more and more expensive tastes. He did not care what anything cost. He realized he needed his salary and decided to begin working again.

In the summer of 1985, ABC offered to renew Geraldo's contract for three more years, but with no raise. Geraldo wanted at least a token raise, but the network would not even give him that. "Take it or leave it," they said. Geraldo realized he had to take it and he said okay. But while the contract was being drawn up, he got himself into even more trouble. His boss, Roone Arledge, had refused to air a piece that his colleague, Sylvia Chase, had done about Marilyn Monroe and her ties to the Kennedys shortly before her death. Arledge was friends with the Kennedys and Geraldo accused him of bad journalism. Though Sylvia asked him not to risk his career for her sake, Geraldo was always one to voice his opinion, and loudly at that. This time, he did even more. In a telephone interview with syndicated columnist Liz Smith, Geraldo publicly denounced his boss and committed professional suicide.

"I stood in my kitchen and made headlines," says Geraldo. "Stoked with moral fury, I charged

He did all this to make a point and show ABC how much they'd miss him if he were gone. "Unfortunately," Geraldo says, "nobody seemed to care."

"I stood in my kitchen and made headlines," says Geraldo. "Stoked with moral fury, I charged Roone with cronyism and censorship."

GERALDO RIVERA

Roone with cronyism [showing favor to friends] and censorship, and questioned his journalistic integrity. In the process, I burned the already rickety bridge connecting me with my onetime friend and longtime employer." After he spoke out on the issue, he realized that ABC had yet to deliver his new contract.

A series of explosive run-ins over the next few months sealed his fate. Eventually, ABC asked him to resign. His last *20/20* show was on Thursday, November 21, 1985, when Geraldo signed off with the following words:

"Sixteen years ago, I was a long-haired store-front lawyer challenging the system on behalf of my clients. It was exciting, frustrating, passionate stuff and I expected it to be my life's work. Then something totally unexpected happened. I got discovered. Standing on a ghetto street representing a group of demonstrators, I was approached by a reporter who told me ABC was actually interested in putting me on the air, making me a newsman. Two thousand stories and a lifetime later, I've come to the point where it's time for another change. For now at least, I'm going to be leaving *20/20*. As one of the founding members of this wonderful program, this is one of the toughest decisions I have ever made. But it's time to go. I've always been sort of a square peg trying to squeeze into the round hole of network news . . ." At the time, Geraldo was not permitted to discuss his resignation or the settlement he received from ABC.

Geraldo says he felt as if he had lost half of his identity when he lost his job at ABC News. "For fifteen years the second half of my name had been 'ABC News.' It would come out by reflex: 'Geraldo Rivera, ABC News.' (It still does, sometimes.) And so, on December 15, 1985, the day I was removed from the ABC News payroll, I also lost part of my identity. It was the first time since I was fourteen years old that I was without a job." And though millions of people are fired from their jobs yearly, Geraldo lost his job in public. He was being taken off the air. He was understandably depressed.

His agent, Jim Griffin at the William Morris Agency, went looking for new jobs for Geraldo. But there were no offers. Jim finally came up with an offer from Tribune Broadcasting to host a live, syndicated special called "The Mystery of Al Capone's Vault." Jim said the job was belittling, but Geraldo needed the money. "What if there's nothing in the vault?" Jim asked. "You'll be humiliated on national TV."

Geraldo didn't care. "How much?" he asked. "Twenty-five thousand," Jim replied.

Geraldo says he felt as if he had lost half of his identity when he lost his job at ABC News.

GERALDO RIVERA

"Ask for fifty and I'll take it," Geraldo said. The job would buy him some time while he looked for other offers.

As it turned out, there was nothing in Al Capone's vault after all. Geraldo was afraid he looked like a fool on national TV again. But at the conclusion of the show he had many new job offers waiting for him. His Al Capone special had broken all records for television ratings. His ratings were through the roof. His career was not over. Not by a long shot. Whatever Geraldo did would draw a big audience. There was no doubt the public still loved him.

Geraldo looked over all the offers and decided that he would accept the one from Tribune Entertainment to do a daytime talk show. In the meantime, he became a special contributor to *Entertainment Tonight*.

In July 1987, Geraldo married C. C. Dyer, his associate producer from *20/20*, for what he now adamantly claims will be his last marriage. Sadly, his father passed away at Thanksgiving that same year.

His own talk show, *Geraldo*, began in 1987 and continues to be a success. Using much the same format as he had for *Eyewitness News*, Geraldo has a devoted following of TV viewers who love his independent reporting and lack of con-

Whatever Geraldo did would draw a big audience. There was no doubt the public still loved him.

cern with convention. He is still criticized by traditional journalists who do not like his style; but he is widely admired by his adoring public. "Well, I really only care about my viewers," Geraldo admits.

Lilly Rivera is still alive and recently celebrated her seventy-fifth birthday. The family had a very large reunion on New Year's of 1995, with both sides gathering in Puerto Rico. Geraldo has remained close with Gabriel over the years, even though Gabriel lives with his mother on the West Coast. "I fly to California for work several times each month," Geraldo says,

Geraldo and wife, C. C., taken in 1991

"and I'm able to see a lot of him. I recently met his new girlfriend and we're discussing whether he should attend college in the east or the west. Of course, I would rather he went to college closer to me so I can see him more."

GERALDO RIVERA

On November 7, 1992, after five long years of "trying everything," Geraldo and C. C. were blessed with the birth of a baby girl, Isabella, that they had hoped for. C. C. and Geraldo were never sure their dream of having children would come true. "Then, we were about to return to the fertility specialist for a second baby when C. C. got pregnant again, this time the old-fashioned way," says Geraldo with delight. Simone was born on September 24, 1994. After many years in Manhattan, Geraldo, C. C., Isabella, and Simone now call New Jersey home.

Geraldo's talk show began on the air in 1987.

When questioned about whom he admires most in broadcast journalism, Geraldo is quick to state, "Phil Donahue, because he created the talk-show format; Barbara Walters, Diane Sawyer, Dan Rather, and Hugh Downs are also wonderful in this business." While he readily admits that too many talk shows walk a fine line between journalism and freak shows, he wants his show to be fascinating, interesting, innovative, and entertaining without pandering to the worst aspects of American society. He feels he is in the business of change; he is most happy if he can take a bad situation and make it better.

"Daytime shows can sometimes be freak shows, especially during the sweeps months [when ratings are very important]. What you try to do is walk a line between being commercially competitive on one hand, and pandering on the other hand. I think that I do that more success-

Geraldo with some audience members on his talk show

fully than most, although I'm still trying to live down the stereotype that resulted from my 1988 brawl with the skinheads. [People] see me as a metaphor for violence on camera now. I don't think that's fair at all, and it has nothing to do with the facts," Geraldo says. "It's easy to use me as an example; I have instant name recognition."

He was sorry to hear about the murder that resulted from a 1995 *Jenny Jones* show, after which a guest murdered an acquaintance who had appeared on the show as his "secret admirer."

Geraldo and his father, Cruz Rivera, taken in 1980 at the Puerto Rican Day Parade dinner

"I don't think that the *Jenny Jones* catastrophe was that much of an unforeseen development," Geraldo says. "It's almost a logical result of some pretty irresponsible producing. And if they keep upping the ante as to what is expected, then you're going to have more of these tragedies, not less of them. You've got to be a lot more professional about finding out who your guests are. A little research by those involved with *Jenny Jones* would have probably turned up something suspicious about this character that could've been a warning signal of his behavior. You're setting up a person in that situation. It's not to suggest that the program is responsible for this man's going out there and choosing a gun as an alternative; but it is to suggest that when you have amateurs out there playing with people's lives, tragedies can sometimes result."

In 1994 and 1995, Geraldo was very happy to be back at his investigative reporting, doing a live commentary about the O.J. Simpson trial for CNBC on a new show called *Rivera Live*. "This is what I do best," Geraldo tells us. "This is what I'm good at. Some of my loudest critics now admit that I am one of the best investigative reporters."

In addition to his first love, investigative reporting, Geraldo enjoys all active sports. He is an avid sailor; he enjoys his boat and the sea. A boxing fan, he owns the Broadcast Boxing Club in Manhattan. He also owns a newspaper called *The Two River Times*, of which he is very proud. It is a weekly newspaper in Monmouth County, New Jersey. In 1995, the paper won first prize for investigative reporting from the New Jersey Press Association for a long-running exposé about a quadruple arson/murder where four released mental patients were burned to death in their townhouse. The crime was never solved until his newspaper got involved.

"Some of my loudest critics now admit that I am one of the best investigative reporters."

GERALDO RIVERA

For those who would like to follow in his footsteps to a career in broadcast journalism, Geraldo has this advice: "Get practical experience early. Get into broadcasting as soon as you possibly can, as an intern or gopher or in any

Geraldo enjoys amateur boxing, and he owns the Broadcast Boxing Club in Manhattan.

entry-level position you can find. Get yourself in the door so you can learn from the people actually doing it. The people actually doing it know far more than those who are teaching it." And if you do become a success, Geraldo advises, "Don't ever forget where you came from."

Geraldo stands in front of the well-known signature for his talk show.

▼▼▼▼▼▼
And if you do become a success, Geraldo advises, "Don't ever forget where you came from."
▲▲▲▲▲▲

MELISSA EVE GONZALEZ

Actress
1980-

"I f you want something badly enough, you should go for it. If you believe it in your heart, it can happen for you.**"**

Melissa Gonzalez, as told to Barbara Marvis, March 1995

BIO HIGHLIGHTS

- Born August 19, 1980, in Chicago, Illinois; mother: Everlidis Rivera Rojas; stepfather: Miguel Rojas
- Resides in Humboldt Park section of Chicago
- Attends Lincoln Park High School in Chicago
- Became involved with the Happiness Club in 1993; travels around Chicago performing original skits, plays, and songs that give positive messages to youth
- Selected in 1994 by Children's Television Workshop to play "Gaby" on their *Ghostwriter* series, shown weekly on PBS

Ever since she was nine years old and performed in her first talent show, Melissa has dreamed of making acting her career.

MELISSA GONZALEZ

From the parks and schools around Chicago, Illinois, to the television studios in New York City, Melissa Gonzalez is just as comfortable performing before a live audience as she is in front of a TV camera. Ever since she was nine years old and performed in her first talent show at school, Melissa has dreamed of making acting her career. She loves entertaining people and making them smile. Though her number-one priority is to finish her education, including college, she is looking forward to a full-time career in acting; and with her recent performance on PBS's *Ghostwriter*, she is certainly on the right track. "I love to act," says Melissa. "It gives me a chance to express my feelings and pretend to be someone other than who I am. It's so much fun."

Born on August 19, 1980, in Chicago, Illinois, Melissa Eve Gonzalez is the only daughter of Everlidis Rivera Rojas (Abby) and her stepfather, Miguel Rojas. She has a younger brother, Miguel, Jr., born in 1988 (Melissa calls him Meto). Her mother was born and raised in Chicago to parents of Puerto Rican descent. She is a full-time homemaker. Melissa explains that her mother's name is actually "Evy," but no one seemed to understand Evy when she told them her name. People just assumed she said "Abby," and so she became Abby. Her stepfather was born in Santo

Domingo, in the Dominican Republic, and immigrated to the United States when he was ten years old. He is currently an auto body mechanic instructor for Coyne American Institute.

Miguel and Abby met at a dance nearly fifteen years ago, and they have been happily married ever since. Melissa describes her relationship with her parents as very close and loving. Her parents are very supportive of her career choice and they help her in every way they can. Melissa considers herself lucky to have such wonderful parents and a happy home to grow up in. Though the Humboldt Park section of Chicago sports too much graffiti and boarded-up buildings, the strong support Melissa receives from her family insulates her from

Melissa with her mother, father, and little brother, Meto

MELISSA GONZALEZ

the street violence and the gangs. "Kids need a lot of strong support from their families or else they'll turn to the streets," says Melissa's stepfather. "You can grow up in the ghetto, but you don't have to be a product of it. We believe love and dedication is what makes a good home, not so much the area you live in."

Melissa attended the Christopher Columbus School in Chicago from kindergarten through fourth grade. She attended Jose de Diego Community Academy from fifth until eighth grade. She is currently attending Lincoln Park High School in Chicago. Melissa loves happy times, and so it is not surprising that her favorite TV shows are cartoons.

Melissa loved visiting Disney World for the first time when she was six. Here she is in Florida on August 19, 1986

Her fondest memory is of the first time she visited Disney World in Florida. Her parents took her for her sixth birthday, and she actually got to hug Mickey Mouse. She has enjoyed returning to Florida every few years, and loves to take her little brother to see all the sights in Orlando.

MELISSA GONZALEZ

In 1989, when she was in third grade, Melissa had a chance to participate in a talent show at school. She was too frightened to go on stage by herself, so she choreographed a dance routine with three other girls. "I thought I was going to get booed off the stage," Melissa says. But everyone loved their routine; and Melissa loved the applause. Her mother thought she was good enough to take dance lessons, so she enrolled her at Miss Geri's School of Dance, and her young career got its start. Melissa also takes piano lessons at American Music World from instructor Olivia Coleman.

That summer after third grade, Melissa traveled with her family to her stepfather's homeland in the Dominican Republic. She got to see where Christopher Columbus lived, ate, and slept. She got to meet some of her stepfather's relatives for the first time. Melissa loves to travel and hopes to be able to do a lot more as she gets older. She enjoyed a school trip to Washington, D.C. last year, and she is looking forward to a trip to Hawaii that her mother has promised her when she graduates from high school.

Melissa at eleven years old

MELISSA GONZALEZ

A great deal of Melissa's life revolves around her weekly rehearsals and performances with the Happiness Club. The club, directed by Gigi Harris Faraci, is a performing group of young people who tour around Chicago in the parks and the schools to send positive messages to other young people. Every week on Sunday, from 10:00 A.M. until 4:30 P.M., these young people get together

Melissa performing with the Happiness Club at Daley Plaza in Chicago

to rehearse or perform their original skits, plays, and songs. The club includes youngsters from six to seventeen years old. As Melissa became more involved in the club, she began to think more and more toward an acting career. When she would see other young adults on television shows or in commercials, she was always telling her mother, "I can do that! I'm just as good as she is." But her mother did not quite know how to break her into acting. Melissa and her mother contacted Gigi, the director of the Happiness Club, and Gigi said she could start by getting an agent for Melissa.

In 1994, Gigi led Melissa to the Linda Jack Talent Agency in Chicago, and Mickey Grossman became Melissa's agent. "Melissa knows who she is," says Gigi. "She is very self-assured. She has a deep desire to help others." It was a natural that Mr. Grossman would eventually find parts for Melissa.

He began looking for work for Melissa right away. He got her auditions for parts in television shows and commercials. Most of the auditions began in Chicago, and Melissa auditioned for several parts each week. But there are few parts available for young adults, and there is fierce competition for them. It takes a lot of work sometimes to land one small job. Sometimes, when she was called back for a part, she had to go to New York or Los Angeles. Finally, last year, after a screen test in New York, Melissa was notified that she had a part in the *Ghost-*

A great deal of Melissa's life revolves around her weekly rehearsals and performances with the Happiness Club.

Melissa has her make-up done by Anita on the *Ghostwriter* set in New York.

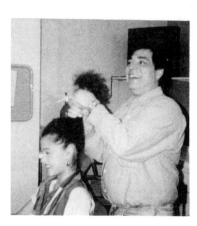

Melissa's hairdresser, Dallas, fixes her hair before she is due on the set.

writer series, a fast-paced, mystery/adventure series on PBS that emphasizes the ability to read as a method to solve neighborhood mysteries. The seven members of the *Ghostwriter* team solve mysteries with the help of an invisible teammate, *Ghostwriter*, who communicates only in writing. He leaves the team clues and messages to help them solve their mysteries. "I was so excited when I got the part," Melissa recalls. "I was jumping for joy!"

Melissa was chosen by Children's Television Workshop to play the part of Gaby on the series after a nationwide talent search in which 450 girls auditioned for the part. The original actress that played Gaby left at the beginning of the third season, and recasting a popular character is a critical decision for any established show. "Melissa was the second actress I saw, and my immediate reaction was 'That's Gaby!'" commented *Ghostwriter's* executive producer Liz Nealon. "She delivers the 'real kid' feeling that's so important to the *Ghostwriter* ensemble cast. She's poised, intelligent, genuine, and bilingual," said Nealon. "Everything we could have hoped for in a new regular."

Her mother and brother accompanied Melissa to New York for the two months she had to film the series. Her stepfather visited several times over July and August, but he had to work, so she missed being with him for the summer vacation. She reported for the first day on the job on July 6, 1994. That morning there was a photo shoot on the set and she got to meet the entire

cast. "It was so exciting," says Melissa. "All the people were so nice to me. And it was so much fun because everyone else was my age, too."

"Every morning, I had to report to the studio by 7:00 A.M., have breakfast, report to ward-

Melissa's family joined her in New York for a little sightseeing. Left to right: Mom, Melissa, Dad, Meto, Grandma Sergia, and Aunt Marionela.

MELISSA GONZALEZ

Melissa filming 'Four Days of the Cockatoo"

robe and get dressed, get my hair and makeup done, read through the script and rehearse with the other cast members, and get ready to work! It was much different than performing before a live audience like I do for the Happiness Club, because if you make a mistake, they just go back and reshoot it since it is on tape. If you mess up live on stage, it is so embarrassing."

Melissa says she had the most fun on the set of *Ghostwriter* when they were filming the storyline called "The Attack of the Slime Monster." In this four-part episode, the team writes an origi-

Katie Couric joined the *Ghostwriter* team as host of the *Ghostwriter* "Three-Peat Special."

nal story. As they gather around the computer, writing, revising, and thinking aloud, the action that they are imagining comes alive on screen. "I got slimed," she remembers. "And I got stuck in a big purple cocoon, and dragged in a wagon by a little slime monster." Yet, with all the fun she had in New York, she found it most difficult to be separated from her other relatives for the two-month period. Melissa has grandparents, seven aunts, two uncles, and ten cousins just on her mother's side, who live nearby in Chicago. She is very close to them, and when filming was over, she was glad to be back home with her family again.

Since the summer of 1994, Melissa has continued to audition regularly and to perform with the Happiness Club. She has done one voice-over job, which she also enjoyed (a voice-over is where she speaks for a cartoon character). She also began high school in 1995, which was quite exciting, but a big adjustment. She graduated from eighth grade with honors and received awards for perfect attendance, honor roll, peer helper, band, good conduct, and excellence in reading and math. She hopes to have a repeat performance in high school and go on to college. She loves having a little brother; that is, except when he gets in her room and messes up her things! When Melissa is not acting or going to school,

Melissa, who plays "Gaby," and David Lopez, who plays her on-screen brother, "Alex," encounter mystery and danger when they try to save "Calypso," an endangered bird.

she enjoys dancing, playing the piano, rollerblading, reading, and having fun with her friends.

Melissa gets slimed in the episode "Attack of the Slime Monster."

She admires Julia Roberts and Tom Hanks and enjoyed seeing the movie *Forrest Gump.* And of all the shows on television, Melissa enjoys watching cartoons, especially *Rocko's Modern Life* and *Rugrats.*

Both of Melissa's parents are bilingual and so she understands Spanish perfectly. She also believes in bilingual education in the schools. "I think Hispanic immigrants should be taught in Spanish when they first come to the United States and are trying to learn English," Melissa says.

Melissa Gonzalez

"After a few years of being exposed to the new language, they can then be taught in English."

Melissa advises all young people to stay in school. "Don't do drugs or gangs," she says, "because these won't get you your dreams."

"Melissa gives so much of herself, it is natural that good things have happened to her. She really splurges on life," says Gigi Harris Faraci.

"The most remarkable trait about Melissa," says agent Mickey Grossman, "is that in all the notoriety she has received, it has not gone to her head. She has handled the situation like most other things in her life – as just another challenge to conquer." With her determination and support from a loving family, Melissa is sure to have a bright and happy future ahead of her.

The *Ghostwriter* team from left to right, back to front: Blaze Berdahl, David Lopez, Sheldon Turnipseed, Melissa Gonzalez, Lateaka Vinson, William Hernandez, and Tram-Anh Tran

FEDERICO PEÑA

Lawyer, Mayor, U.S. Secretary of Transportation

1947-

"Try to understand other people's points of view. On one hand, we are really all the same, but on the other, we all have our differences. We were all brought up differently depending on our family circumstances and where we're from, but we must understand other people's backgrounds and differences. Basically, we are all one family. "

Federico Peña, as told to Barbara Marvis, April 1995

BIO HIGHLIGHTS

- Born March 15, 1947, in Laredo, Texas; mother: Lucia Farias Peña; father: Gustavo Peña
- Grew up in Brownsville, Texas
- Graduated from University of Texas at Austin with B.A. degree in 1969
- Received Juris Doctor in 1972 from University of Texas School of Law
- Licensed to practice law in both Texas and Colorado
- Was Civil Rights lawyer in Colorado
- Elected to the Colorado House of Representatives in 1978
- Elected Mayor of Denver in 1983
- Appointed U.S. Secretary of Transportation for President Bill Clinton in 1993
- Currently: married to Ellen Hart; two children, Cristina and Nelia

FEDERICO PEÑA

In May of 1994, Federico Peña spoke at the commencement ceremonies at the University of Texas, the same college where he had earned his degree in 1969. "For me, coming back tonight brings back memories of 1967," he told the graduating class of 1994. "The Longhorns had a great team that year . . . the Beatles had a great new album out . . . And Mickey Mouse was running for student body president, right here on this campus, near this building.

"A small group of students . . . was restless. We were tired of campus politics, as usual, and we knew a lot of other students felt the same way. So, we entered Mickey Mouse as a candidate for student body president. We made a papier-mâché Mickey Mouse head and rounded out the uniform with a blue blazer, white pants, white turtleneck, and white gloves – and we started campaigning . . . I remember it well – I was Mickey Mouse . . .

"So, there I was, a short, cocky, protest candidate from Texas with a squeaky voice and giant ears – years ahead of Ross Perot. And as a matter of fact, we did so well that one of the other candidates came up to me one day and tried to make a deal for my support. She asked me, 'What do you want?'

"I said: 'More cheese, bigger holes, no mouse traps . . .' It was all a bit silly, maybe

"We entered Mickey Mouse as a candidate for student body president."

even cynical. But we had a lot of fun, we came in third, and we shook up campus politics.

"And that turned out to be the beginning of a long journey in politics for me, a journey that quickly grew very serious, not so funny at all, as it passed through the antiwar movement, and the struggle for civil rights, and on into elective politics in Colorado, and the mayor's office in Denver, and now to the position of a cabinet secretary for President Clinton."

This string of events is really not unexpected given that Federico Peña comes from a family that has been in public life in Texas for over two hundred years. He has always been regarded as utterly scrupulous, and a man of his word.

Federico Fabian Peña was born on March 15, 1947, in Laredo, Texas, of Mexican descent. He was the third of six children born to Gustavo and Lucia (Farias) Peña. The three children born after Federico were triplets. He has four brothers and one sister: Gustavo is the oldest, then Oscar, Federico, and the triplets, Alfredo, Ana, and Alberto. They grew up in Brownsville, Texas.

His father, Gustavo, was a broker for a cotton manufacturer. One of Federico's great-grandfathers served as mayor of Laredo during the Civil War. Another great-grandfather was a

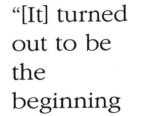

"[It] turned out to be the beginning of a long journey into politics for me . . ."

His parents put all six of their children through college.

member of the first school board in Laredo. His grandfather was an alderman in Laredo for almost twenty-five years.

His parents put all six of their children through college. Over time, they raised three lawyers, an accountant, an assistant high-school principal, and a teacher. Federico remembers as a teenager sweeping cotton dust from the floor of his father's office. He poured concrete at construction jobs he held in the summer, and shoveled sorghum in a grain elevator. He worked through college, too, washing dishes at one of the girls' dormitories and cooking hamburgers in a nearby restaurant.

Peña tells us that his parents taught him respectfulness, perseverance, loyalty, and to strive for high standards. His parents encouraged outstanding performance, both in sports and in intellectual pursuits. The Peña children addressed their parents as "sir" and "ma'am." They were punished for showing disrespect or for swearing. The family spoke both Spanish and English at home, as did most of the families in Brownsville, where Hispanics make up nearly 85 percent of the population. At the supper table, they often talked about politics and civic responsibility.

All five of the Peña brothers were altar boys at the Sacred Heart Catholic Church in Brownsville. Federico attended St. Joseph's Academy, a local high school. He says he had to work harder than other students to get good grades, and he never scored well on standardized tests. He was, however, named "most likely to succeed" by his graduating class of 1964.

He enrolled at the University of Texas, at Austin, and received a B.A. degree in 1969. The University of Texas was a major adjustment for him. There was a large Latino population in Brownsville, but the University of Texas was largely white. "There were no minorities on campus," Federico remembers. "I ran into clear discrimination. There were people who wouldn't talk to me." Federico learned quickly to deal with the outside world.

He then attended the University of Texas School of Law and received his Juris Doctor degree in 1972. His brother Alfredo had been practicing law in Denver, Colorado; after Federico visited him there, he decided that he would move there and form a law partnership with his brother. He passed the Colorado Bar exams and the two brothers established Peña and Peña in 1973.

From 1972 to 1974, Federico served as a staff lawyer for the Mexican American Legal Defense and Education Fund. He handled police brutality cases and sought voting rights for Hispanics.

▼▼▼▼▼▼

"There were no minorities on campus," Federico remembers. "I ran into clear discrimination. There were people who wouldn't talk to me."

▲▲▲▲▲▲

"The overall perception was that the Hispanic community was not being fully embraced by the educational system and by the broader community."

FEDERICO PEÑA

Then he became a legal adviser for the Chicano Education Project. He fought very hard during this time for bilingual education and for better funding in public schools in Hispanic neighborhoods.

One of the most rewarding experiences Federico remembers while he was practicing law was when he brought suit on behalf of Hispanic children in a school district in Colorado. The parents there felt their children were not receiving an equal opportunity for education. At the same time, he represented several Hispanic educators who felt that there was discrimination in both hiring and promotion practices within their school district. "I got to raise the issue in the community that there was a problem," Federico recently said. "The overall perception was that the Hispanic community was not being fully embraced by the educational system and the broader community. I liked helping the students gain access to an equal education because this was a situation where everyone would win. These children could be more productive members of society with a better education."

Working with the Hispanic community made Federico decide that he would like to enter politics. In 1978, when he was only thirty-one years old, he sought a seat in the Colorado House of

Representatives. He was successful on his very first try. He was named outstanding House Democratic freshman by the Colorado Social Action Committee. He was reelected in 1980. The House then elected him their minority leader during his second term. In 1981, he was voted the outstanding legislator of the year. During his terms in office, he served on the House judiciary, finance, legal services, and rules committees.

In 1982, Federico decided he would not run for reelection in the House. Instead, he announced his candidacy for the mayor of Denver, against William McNichols, Jr., who had been mayor of Denver for the previous fourteen years. No one in Denver even knew who Federico Peña was at the time. But one thing was sure: no one was giving any thought to his pursuit of the mayor's office. His obviously Hispanic surname meant that no one would give him a chance. Denver's Hispanic population was only 18 percent at the time, and almost everyone believed his chances were hopeless.

Six months later, Federico proved everyone wrong. In a bipartisan election, the voters chose the thirty-six-year-old Peña to be their forty-first mayor. He became one of the youngest mayors in the country at the time, and Denver's first

▼▼▼▼▼▼
Working with the Hispanic community made Federico decide he would like to enter politics.
▲▲▲▲▲▲

Several of
his
challengers
tried to
make an
issue over
his Hispanic
background.

FEDERICO PEÑA

Mexican American mayor. It happened with the largest voter turnout in Denver history. Peña had campaigned relentlessly. He had an astonishing number of volunteers – four thousand by many counts. They undertook a drive to register Hispanics and the poor to vote. Many of these people had never voted before because they believed their vote did not count or that they could not make a difference. Because he had worked so publicly with the minority population, he was already well known in their communities. The voters were tired of their old mayor and they wanted a change. Federico Peña was single, young, and dynamic, and the people of Denver liked to think of themselves in those terms. They liked to be associated with Peña.

Several of his challengers tried to make an issue over his Hispanic background. Peña put together a vision of Denver that was so enticing, he reduced the issue of his Hispanic background to a nonissue. He focused on themes of leadership. He said that a mayor had to be more than a manager; that a mayor also had to be a leader, a policy maker, an advocate, a catalyst, an innovator, a promoter, and a mediator. He campaigned with the slogan, "Denver: Imagine a Great City." He also conducted a positive campaign and was considered extremely ethical. During the mayoral race runoff, former District

Attorney Dale Tooley, who was running against Peña, had to cancel his last day of campaigning because his mother had a heart attack. Peña canceled his last day, as well.

Peña was very idealistic when he first took office as mayor. He wanted to make Denver the great city he told everyone about. He proposed a new style of governing with an open-door policy, which meant that he would be available to anyone. He wanted the residents of Denver to be able to contact him directly, so he had his telephone number listed. But there were too many late-night crank calls that interrupted his sleep and he had to discontinue this policy. Peña wanted to be liked by everyone, but not everyone liked what he did. Some of his policies were the subject of much debate at various city council meetings throughout Denver. Mayor Peña could not bear to watch some of the proceedings when he was criticized. "It's taken me time to understand there will always be someone who opposes me," he admitted to Ann Carnahan of *The Rocky Mountain News*. "I have to learn to be a little more thick-skinned, yet not become an insensitive armadillo."

Federico Peña had grand plans for new construction in Denver. He pushed for the building of a new convention center at Denver's Union Station. That proposal was overwhelm-

In a bipartisan election, the voters chose the thirty-six-year-old Peña to be their forty-first mayor.

He had a dream for making Denver a major trade and commercial center in the next century, so he proposed building a new, very modern airport.

FEDERICO PEÑA

ingly defeated in a public referendum. Then the economy in Denver declined, and this undermined Peña's efforts to revitalize the city. There was a slump in oil, mining, and high-technology industries in the mid-1980's that hit Denver very hard. Unemployment went up. Real estate prices fell, and the wonderful things that Peña envisioned for Denver did not happen. By the time he ran for reelection in 1987, his popularity had shrunk to an all-time low. His critics called him an ineffective and indecisive mayor. He was challenged by Don Bain, a Republican lawyer. The election looked very close. Denver finally decided to give Peña a little more time to bring change to the city. On June 16, he won reelection with 51 percent of the vote.

In December 1987, a blizzard and ice storm struck Denver. Peña was vacationing in Mexico when it happened. The city was unable to clear many streets in a timely manner. Some neighborhood streets were still impassable as late as February 1988. This prompted a group of angry citizens to launch a recall drive. The drive ultimately fell two thousand votes short of enough signatures to force a vote, and Peña remained mayor.

During his second term, Mayor Peña was able to get on with some of the expansion program he had promised. He had a dream for making Denver a major trade and commercial center in the next century, so he proposed building a new, very modern airport. The airport was to be located on fifty-three square miles of prairie, eighteen miles northeast of Denver. The new airport was to be designed to handle heavy traffic in bad weather. Because of Denver's location, many flights passed through it, and winter weather caused delays throughout the United States.

Many local leaders opposed the idea of the new airport. They said it was too large and too extravagant. They said the existing airport was sufficient. United Airlines, Denver's main carrier, also opposed the project. But Mayor Peña won approval for the new airport and construction began. The airport

Federico Peña and his wife Ellen are leaving the polls in Denver, Colorado after casting their votes to build the new airport.

was originally scheduled to open in late 1993. However, the airport encountered several problems that delayed the opening. The most notable problem was with a new, high-tech baggage conveyor system that was supposed to speed baggage from the airplanes to the waiting passengers. The new system "chewed up baggage and spit it out," and the system had to

His administration revitalized neighborhoods, planted thousands of trees, cleaned up streets, erased graffiti, repaired abandoned homes, fixed bridges and roads, and built new libraries.

FEDERICO PEÑA

undergo extensive repairs before it could be used. The new airport finally opened in early 1995, and immediately began to show benefits by reducing delays related to foul weather. Indeed, on opening day, three planes simultaneously landed on adjacent runways in snowy weather – the first time this had been done anywhere.

A new convention center was also finally built, as Mayor Peña had proposed during his first term. He brought major-league baseball back to Denver with the Colorado Rockies. His administration revitalized neighborhoods, planted thousands of trees, cleaned up streets, erased graffiti, repaired abandoned homes, fixed bridges and roads, and built new libraries. With the economy heading toward recovery, Peña became popular once again. In 1991, however, he chose not to seek a third term. He said he wanted to spend more time with his family. In May 1988, Federico had married Ellen Hart, a talented distance runner and Harvard-educated lawyer, whom he had met at the 1984 Mayor's Cup Race. On July 22, 1990, Ellen and Federico's first daughter, Nelia, was born. In February 1992, Cristina was born.

After he left the mayor's office, Federico founded Peña Investment Advisors. His company provided pension management. He hired talented Hispanic lawyers and business experts. He also served as a member of a Colorado state commission that worked on a twenty-year trans-

portation plan. The plan detailed long-term construction of mass transit facilities, bike paths, and walkways.

In 1992, Federico Peña headed President Bill Clinton's transition team for transportation issues. Clinton was impressed by Peña's ability to win approval for the Denver airport and by his experience with transportation issues, so he nominated Peña to become secretary for the United States Department of Transportation. At a Sen-

Secretary Peña presents the team award to Lewis Vinciguerra of the U.S. Coast Guard at the Secretary's 27th Annual Award Program, December 1994.

"We are
about
building
bridges, not
bureaucracy;
picking
priorities,
not pork;
moving
people, not
paper; and
above all,
ensuring
travelers'
safety."

FEDERICO PEÑA

ate confirmation hearing before the Senate Commerce, Science, and Transportation Committee, Peña discussed his plans for repairing and rebuilding the nation's infrastructure. He was confirmed by the Senate on January 21, 1993. Since assuming his cabinet position, Secretary Peña has taken a hands-on approach to shaping all aspects of American transportation policy. His vision for the Transportation Department is to ensure travelers' safety, open avenues to trade, and make government more responsive to its citizens by stripping overlapping bureaucracies.

With more than 103,000 employees and an estimated budget of $38.5 billion in fiscal year 1995, the Department of Transportation (DOT) has responsibility for nine administrations. Those administrations control highways, civil aviation, mass transit, railroads, commercial use of outer space, the merchant marine, and the safety of waterways, ports, and oil and gas pipelines. The DOT also oversees the United States Coast Guard. When Peña assumed his position in 1993, the Department had more than 107,000 employees. He trimmed his workforce by 4,000 positions at a savings of $250 million per year. He proposed a new DOT, endorsed by the previous Republican administrations, in which he proposed to cut his workforce by 50 percent from 1992 levels, reduce the number of agencies from ten to three, and corporatize the air traffic control system. "We are about building bridges, not bureaucracy," said Secretary Peña; "picking priorities, not pork; moving people, not paper; and above all, ensuring travelers' safety."

Federico Peña moved quickly to take charge and meet challenges. As soon as he was in office, he helped launch a drive to revitalize the airline industry. On March 15, 1993, he approved a request by British Airways to invest in USAir Group, Inc., giving them the right to own as much as 19.9 percent of USAir. This influx of cash was greatly needed for USAir. But Peña warned that his approval was contingent upon

Secretary Peña is greeted by Rear Admiral Richard Herr and Cmdr. Mark Mayne as he arrives at Coast Guard Air Station Los Angeles, the day of the earthquake. (January 1994)

Secretary Peña advises all young adults to have confidence in themselves and to set goals higher than what they think they can achieve.

FEDERICO PEÑA

Great Britain's willingness to allow American aircraft greater access to airport facilities in Great Britain. He has considered many ways to help the airlines, including tax relief and loan guarantees.

In January 1994, Peña was on the scene shortly after the earthquake in Los Angeles, California. In his hands-on style, he rolled up his sleeves and got right to work. He approved a federal contract to remove crumpled concrete from the devastated area.

Secretary Peña focused national attention on commercial truck and bus safety at a gathering in Kansas City, where government and industry together developed and adopted safety initiatives to remove outdated regulations.

In mass transit, Secretary Peña requested one of the largest budget commitments in U.S. history to help speed commuting, ease traffic, and clean the air. He also has DOT participating in the Technology Reinvestment Project that supports "dual use" and purely civilian research and development by defense contractors. Peña believes that these initiatives will create new American industries and provide high-wage jobs for American workers. Secretary Peña says that investment in transportation is one way to revive America's economy and to enable American companies to compete, and win, in the world economy. He believes that America is in the

Secretary Peña inspects truck during Customer Service Day, October 1994.

midst of a technological revolution in transportation that will create whole new industries. He intends to see DOT play a lead role in many developments, and his persistence has made the Department of Transportation an aggressive, "get-things-done" agency.

Secretary Peña advises all young adults to have confidence in themselves and to set goals higher than what they think they can achieve. "Be confident that you can excel in any en-

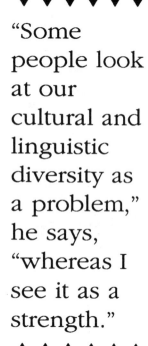

▼▼▼▼▼▼

"Some people look at our cultural and linguistic diversity as a problem," he says, "whereas I see it as a strength."

▲▲▲▲▲▲

FEDERICO PEÑA

deavor, if you work hard enough," he says. "Be as inquisitive as possible and try to learn about many subjects and areas of interest. Constantly challenge yourself to do something you think you cannot do. Always set high goals for yourself. Above all, devote all of your energy and attention to your education. Go to school each day excited about learning something new. Prepare yourself for your academic program. Do your homework and read, read, read – as much as you can in your spare time. If you have the option of goofing off or reading, read a book."

Federico believes that the diversity in our country is a strength. "Some people look at our cultural and linguistic diversity as a problem," he says, "whereas I see it as an asset. Our citizens speak many different languages. Our number-one priority should be to see that all children become fluent in English; but, as a nation, we are more globally competitive if we are multilingual. We should not be forcing immigrants to abandon their native languages; instead, we should be encouraging multilingualism and helping children who only speak English to learn other languages as well. We need bilingual and multicultural education in our schools. It is very important to us, as a nation, that we understand other cultures and speak many languages, so we can compete in what is rapidly becoming a global economy."

Many people describe Peña as "a nice guy, honest and hard-working." He is currently living with his family in Alexandria, Virginia. When he is not busy with his many projects, he enjoys spending time with his family. "We like to explore with the kids," Secretary Peña says. "We take them on many outdoor activities. We have visited local farms and taken the kids to see the cows, the horses, and the pigs. I play a lot of games, like Legos, with them when I am home, and I also like to read to them every day. Ellen is able to do much more with them since she is home. She takes them on all sorts of outings. They go to museums and parks and concerts for kids."

Peña credits much of his success to his strict but loving upbringing. He strives to excel at everything he undertakes and enjoys every new challenge. But most of all, he is proud of his own background and heritage. He recommends that all young people be proud of their heritage and use it as an asset.

ELLEN OCHOA

Scientist, Astronaut

1958-

"**E**ducation is the key. If you study hard and reach far enough, the possibilities are endless. "

Ellen Ochoa, as told to Barbara Marvis, April 1995

BIO HIGHLIGHTS

- Born May 10, 1958, in Los Angeles, California; mother: Rosanne Deardorff; father: Joseph Ochoa

- Grew up in La Mesa, California

- Attended Grossmont High School in La Mesa; valedictorian of 1975 graduating class

- Earned B.S. degree in 1980 from San Diego State University

- Master's and doctorate in electrical engineering earned from Stanford University

- Named finalist to astronaut program in 1987

- Selected by NASA in January 1990

- Married Coe Fulmer Miles on May 27, 1990

- First space flight in April 1993; first female Hispanic in space

ELLEN OCHOA

"I was really looking forward to that first flight," Ellen says. "It was very exciting and a lot of fun."

In April 1993, Ellen Ochoa blasted off into space aboard the Space Shuttle *Discovery*. Harnessed to her seat, and accompanied by four other astronauts, Ellen waited for the solid rocket boosters to burn out. The ride got a lot smoother when the solid boosters were jettisoned. "I was really looking forward to that first flight," Ellen says. "It was very exciting and a lot of fun. It wasn't scary; it was something I really wanted to do." She loved being weightless and floating around in space. She got to look at Earth from a whole new point of view, a view that only a select few will ever experience firsthand.

But there was a lot of hard work involved, also. "We were busy with the science experiments," Ellen recalls, "deploying and retrieving the science satellite, Spartan, which studied the solar corona. We were in space for nine days, but the time went very quickly. It was a wonderful experience." Her first flight was the culmination of nearly three years of preparation beginning when she joined NASA, Johnson Space Center, in July 1990. She also made history when she became the first female Hispanic astronaut in space.

Ellen Ochoa was born on May 10, 1958, in Los Angeles, California. She was the third of five children born to Rosanne (Deardorff) and Joseph Ochoa, who is of Mexican descent. Her sister

Beth was born in 1954. She finished law school in 1995. Her brother Monte was born in 1957; he currently works for the San Diego City Schools as an instructional media specialist. Her younger brother, Tyler, was born in 1962. He is a law professor in Los Angeles, California. And Ellen's youngest brother, Wilson, born in 1964, is a professional musician who plays the French horn with the Charleston, South Carolina Symphony. Their parents were divorced when Ellen was in junior high school. She grew up with her mother and brothers and sister in La Mesa, California.

Ellen attended Northmont Elementary School. She enjoyed school and always worked very hard. She remembers fifth grade as a particularly enjoyable year. Her teacher divided the class into groups, which formed their own countries. Each group had to set up its own form of government. "It was a little bit different that year from my other years in school," Ellen remembers. "We competed all year long with other countries on various projects. Sometimes, at the end of the day, we would have debates with the other groups, for which you could win points for your country. I

Astronaut Ellen Ochoa is on the Space Shuttle *Atlantis's* aft flight deck after completing an operation at the controls for the Remote Manipulator System. She is working with astronaut David McMonagle.

remember being more interested in school that year than the other years. It was fun having the freedom to pick our own topics for research. It was a very creative year."

Ellen has always believed in the value of a good education. She learned this lesson from her mother at an early age. "We were all encouraged to do whatever we wanted to do," Ellen said. "My mother placed a high premium on going to college." In fact, her mother took college courses for twenty-three years. She earned a triple degree in business, biology, and journalism. Her mother now works at the *San Diego Union Tribune.* "If you stay in school," Ellen told a *Hispanic* magazine interviewer, "you have the potential to achieve what you want in the future. Education increases your career options and gives you a chance for a wide variety of jobs."

One of Ellen's favorite subjects in school was math, but she did well in all her studies. When she was thirteen, she won the San Diego County spelling bee. In junior high, she was named the outstanding seventh- and eighth-grade girl. She attended Grossmont High School in La Mesa, where she was valedictorian of her 1975 graduating class. In high school, she also became an accomplished flutist, and she was recognized by her high school as a top performer. She did not

Ellen at age ten, taken on the first day of sixth grade, September 1968

want to pursue a career in music, however. "I like to eat," Ellen said, adding that she knows too many musicians who have a hard time just paying their bills. Ellen wanted something more secure. "I still play a lot whenever I can on the side, so it's something you can do as a hobby as well."

In 1975, she entered San Diego State University, where she earned a B.S. degree in physics in 1980. Her postgraduate work was done at Stanford University, where she earned a master's degree in 1981 and a doctorate in electrical engineering in 1985. She earned a Stanford engineering fellowship and an IBM predoctoral fellowship. It was actually in graduate school that she first thought about going to work for NASA. Some friends of hers were applying to the astronaut program. They told her how to apply and when applications were being accepted. "So I wrote NASA to get more information," Ellen revealed. "That's when I became very interested in trying to [become an astronaut], because this was the first time I realized that I might be qualified. I really had no idea before then what sort of people NASA looked for or what type of qualifications you needed. This really was not a lifelong ambition. I thought about a lot of different careers over my life, but this turned out to be what I really wanted to do." Ellen applied

It was actually in graduate school that she thought about going to work for NASA.

to NASA in 1985 and was named one of the top one hundred finalists in 1987.

Applying to the astronaut program takes time. So Ellen kept busy with her original career goal of research engineering. After graduation, she landed a job in the Imaging Technology Branch of Sandia National Laboratories in Livermore, California, as a research engineer. She worked at Sandia from 1985 through 1988. At Sandia, Ellen worked on developing optical methods for image processing that are normally done by a computer. One method she helped devise removes noise from an image through an optical system rather than using a standard digital computer to do the work. Before her thirty-third birthday, she held three patents in optical processing.

Ellen and her brothers and sisters shown when Ellen was nine years old. From left to right: Wilson, Ellen, Beth, Tyler, and Monte, taken in November 1967

About this time, Ellen also took on another hobby after her older brother, Monte, got his pilot's license. She decided she would like to learn to fly, too, and to learn more about aviation. In 1988 she got her private pilot's license.

In 1988 Ellen joined the NASA Ames Research Center in Mountain View, California. There she led a research group in optical processing. Her primary work was on optical recognition systems for space automation. Just six months later, she was chosen as Chief of the Intelligent Systems Technology Branch, where she served as the technical and administrative supervisor of thirty-five engineers and scientists. They were engaged in research and development of high performance computational systems for aerospace missions.

Finally, in January 1990, she was selected by NASA for the astronaut program. Her astronaut class included eighteen men and five women. Women had only been included in the astronaut program for a short while. Before 1978, there had been no women astronauts.

The year 1990 was special for Ellen in other ways, too. On May 27, 1990, Ellen married Coe Fulmer Miles of Molalla, Oregon. They met two years earlier when they both worked for NASA, Ames. He is currently a technical adviser for the patent law firm Arnold, White, and Durkee. Together, they enjoy attending concerts and plays, traveling, and exercising.

Did her new husband have any worries about his wife training to be blasted out into space for scientific research? Not according to Ellen. "He thinks my job is exciting," Ellen says. "He is very supportive." Ellen and Coe settled in Houston,

▼▼▼▼▼▼
Before 1978, there had been no women astronauts.
▲▲▲▲▲▲

ELLEN OCHOA

Texas, near the Johnson Space Center when she became an astronaut.

Ellen trained to be a mission specialist and prepared to go on her first space flight. When she was not training, her jobs included representing the crew office for robotics and for flight software. In April 1993, her dream finally came true when she flew as a mission specialist aboard STS-56, carrying the ATLAS-2 (Atmospheric Laboratory for Applications and Science) payload.

She helped with several scientific experiments during her nine-day flight. She used a set of special instruments to measure the chemical composition, temperature, and pressure of Earth's atmosphere. She conducted studies to better understand the effect of solar radiation on Earth's climate and environment. She used the Remote Manipulator System aboard the shuttle to deploy and retrieve the Spartan satellite.

Ellen participated in a survival training course as a part of her astronaut training program.

This satellite was developed to help study the sun's corona. Her experience with robotics helped her with this task.

On November 3, 1994, Ellen was the payload commander on the STS-66, ATLAS-3 mission aboard the Space Shuttle *Atlantis*. In space for eleven days this time, with four other NASA astronauts and a European mission specialist, she continued the series of Spacelab flights to study the energy of the sun during an eleven-year solar cycle. During this flight, an atmospheric research satellite was deployed, and Ellen used the Remote Manipulator System to retrieve the satellite at the end of its eight-day free flight.

Though NASA did at one time deploy commercial communications satellites for private companies from the space shuttle payload bay, Ellen says this is no longer being done. Most commercial satellites are launched from expendable launch vehicles such as Delta, Titan, and Atlas. The shuttle is being used today mostly for scientific research in a wide variety of areas and for development of the international space station. In 1994 and 1995, shuttle missions have included atmospheric research, life sciences, material sciences, and astronomy experiments. NASA is building up to the assembly of the space station. "We have seven flights scheduled in 1995, 1996, and 1997 that will be docking with the Russian space station," Ellen said. "Most of our flights will be involved with life-science experiments and technology demonstrations for the space station. Starting in late 1997, we will begin building the station. This is expected to take

"We have seven flights scheduled in 1995, 1996, and 1997 that will be docking with the Russian space station," Ellen said.

about four to four and a half years. The goal of the space station is to provide a platform where we can perform more interactive experiments than we can currently on the shuttle, and they can last over a longer period of time. There will be people living at the station over long periods of time starting in 1998. Once much of the assembly is done, we can then begin to focus on the scientific experiments to be performed from the space station. That is the overall mission of the international space station.

Ellen wears a training version of the launch and entry suits. She is shown here with astronaut Joseph P. Tanner.

"The first main module that the United States is sending up is the laboratory module. There is also a Russian laboratory module, and there will be European and Japanese laboratory modules there when the whole station is complete. The modules are designed for a ten-year life-span and will be floating in orbit over that period of time. The shuttle will then be used to dock with these orbiting labs and will carry people and equipment to and from the stations," Ellen said. Ellen hopes to be a part of the assembly process for the space station, and she is working on a lot of feasibility studies from the ground now. She also wants to be a part of the experiments being performed once the station is in place.

On the ground, all the astronauts have jobs that support the space program. When she is not preparing for a flight, Ellen works at the Johnson Space Center on the space station program in the area of operations. She evaluates the station from an astronaut's point of view. Some other astronauts work at Cape Canaveral in Florida in support of orbital processing. Ellen also travels around giving talks for NASA about her responsibilities as an astronaut.

Ellen learned how to handle a parachute in case there was an emergency ejection from a jet aircraft.

"The space program provides the American people with a lot of benefits," she said. "The NASA program employs a lot of highly educated, talented, and creative people that we, as a nation, have decided we want to utilize. These people are making great advances in technology and science using their creative talents. Part of our role as a nation is to explore new territories and to understand more about science. If we didn't have an agency such as NASA committed to exploration and scientific development, then I think, overall as a nation, we'd stop growing. We would not be moving forward in areas of technology that we have always wanted to pursue. It would change the whole character

ELLEN OCHOA

of the United States and what we think is important."

NASA has also provided a lot of technology over the years that has been adapted for commercial use, Ellen says, and the American people benefit greatly from the space program research. "Medicine and health care is one area where NASA technology has contributed greatly. A lot of the portable medical equipment in use now derived from advances made by NASA. Patients in remote areas can access doctors via tele-video

Ellen secures herself in a small life raft during an emergency bail-out training exercise.

hookups, where the doctors can diagnose problems without being in the same town as the patient. Some of the imaging technology we use in space to see Earth's resources and land formations has been adapted for use in identifying breast cancer. A lot of areas to do with the environment have also benefited from NASA research. We learned how to clean up contaminated or polluted areas of Earth when we developed the technology to deal with types of pollution or contamination we might encounter in a remote site, such as outer space or another planet."

ELLEN OCHOA

What is Ellen's advice for aspiring young astronauts? "Education is the key to becoming an astronaut," she says. "Some people think you have to learn to fly a plane in order to work for NASA. This is not a requirement, although it is helpful to have aviation experience. A college degree in a scientific or technical area is

what it takes. Whatever else you do, stay in school."

In her spare time, Ellen enjoys volleyball and bicycling. In 1989 she was awarded the Hispanic Engineer National Achievement Award as the Most Promising Engineer in Government. In 1991 she was given the *Hispanic* magazine Science Achievement Award. In 1993 she received the Congressional Hispanic Caucus Medallion of Excellence, and in 1994 she was given the Engineering Achievement Award by Women in Science and Engineering. As of 1995, Ellen Ochoa had logged over 484 hours in space. Someday, we might even hear that Ellen is living in outer space!

Ellen is on the flight deck of the Space Shuttle *Atlantis*, where the six crew members posed for their portrait. Shown from left to right in lower frame: Joseph P. Tanner, Donald McMonagle, Scott Parazynski, and Curtis Brown. Floating at top: Ellen Ochoa and Jean-Francois Clervoy, representing the European Space Agency.

Index

ABOUT THE AUTHOR

Barbara Marvis has been a professional writer for nearly twenty years. Motivated by her own experience with ethnic discrimination as a young Jewish girl growing up in suburban Philadelphia, Ms. Marvis developed the **Contemporary American Success Stories** series to dispel racial and ethnic prejudice, to tell culturally diverse stories that maintain ethnic and racial distinction, and to provide positive role models for young minorities. She is the author of several books for young adults, including **Famous People of Asian Ancestry**. She holds a B.S. degree in English and Communications from West Chester State University, in West Chester, Pennsylvania, and an M.Ed. in remedial reading from the University of Delaware, in Newark, Delaware.

She and her husband, Bob, currently live with their four children in northern Maryland.